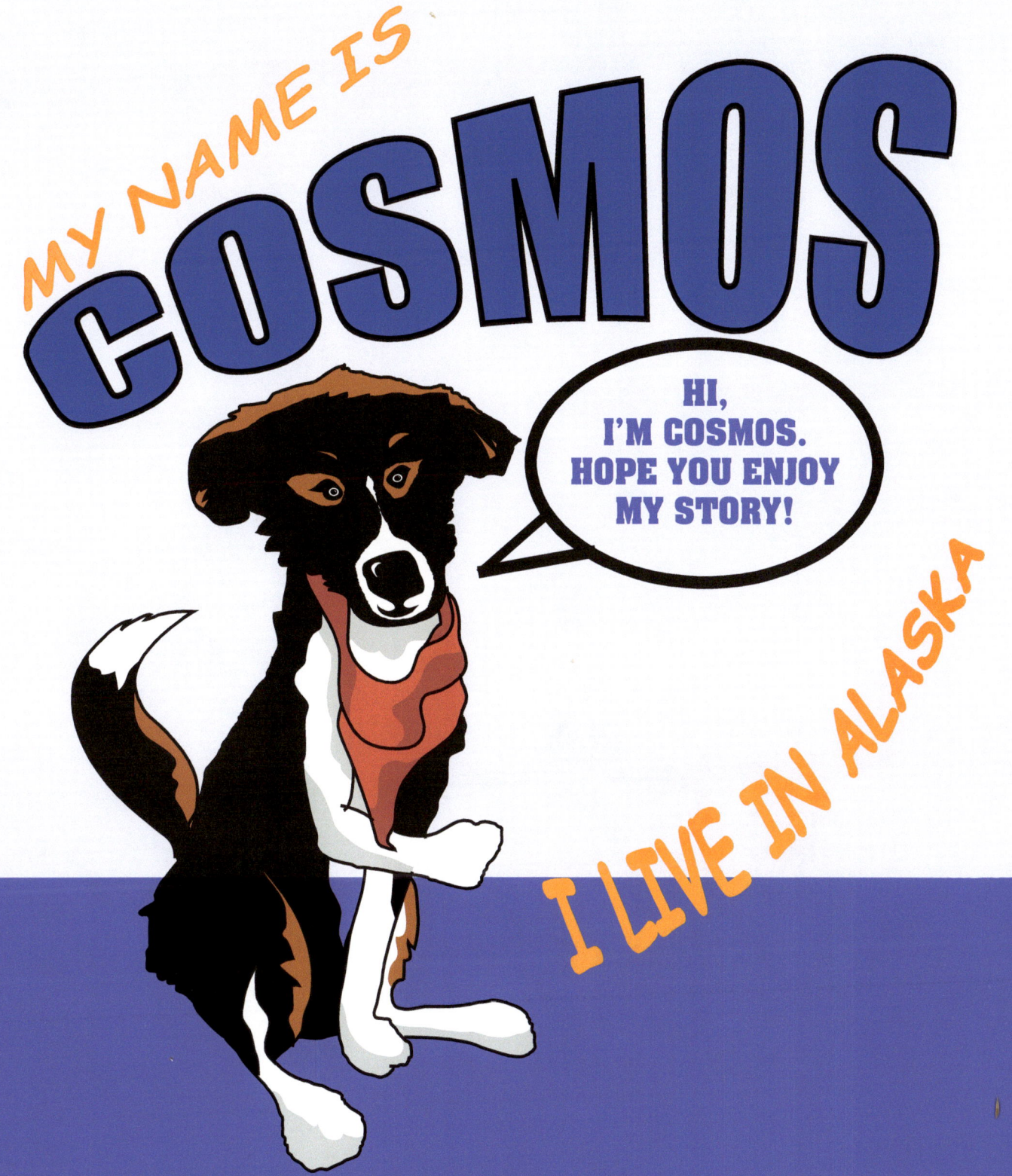

Copyright © 2011 by Weatherholt & Associates, LLC all rights reserved worldwide. No portion of this book may be reproduced or transmitted in any form or by any means, electronic, mechanical, including photocopying, recording, or by any information storage or retrieval system, without the prior written permission of the publisher.

Book Design: David W Weatherholt
Editorial Assistance: Brianna Hammes & Amanda Cullen
Body Typeface: Minion Pro
Pullout Typeface: Aachen Standard Bold

Library of Congress Cataloging-in-Publication Data
Weatherholt, David W.
    My Name is Cosmos I Live in Alaska/
    Written by David W Weatherholt;
    Illustrated by Charles Lindemuth
     1. Cowboys-Juvenile literature.
     2. Dog-Alaska-Juvenile literature.
     3. Life-Arctic Regions-Juvenile literature

ISBN: 978-0-9823041-2-9 (hardcover)
          978-0-9823041-3-6 (softcover)
LCCN: 2010943281

More about the author David W Weatherholt at www.waconsult.com,
email, david@waconsult.com, Twitter; waconsult

More about the illustrator Charles Lindemuth at www.lindemuth.com

Publisher: Weatherholt & Associates, LLC Book Publishing
          10600 Cutter Circle, Anchorage, Alaska 99515-2725
          907.360.9241, www.waconsult.com

Dedicated to my mother who loves all animals!

Alice R. Weatherholt

HELLO, my name is Cosmos and I live in Alaska, the Last Frontier! Now you may think that I don't look like a sled dog.

You sure would be **RIGHT** about that! I am a mixed breed—Bernese Mountain Dog and Border Collie—sometimes called cowboy dogs. We make great cattle herding dogs.

I was born with two brothers and a sister on a ranch in the West—a place far, far away from Alaska. You may be wondering how I got to Alaska. Listen closely.... and I will tell you my **STORY**.

ended here

My master **DAVE** lives in Alaska. Dave was looking for a special dog. His sister Sharon lived in cattle ranching country and told him that she would find him an awesome dog.

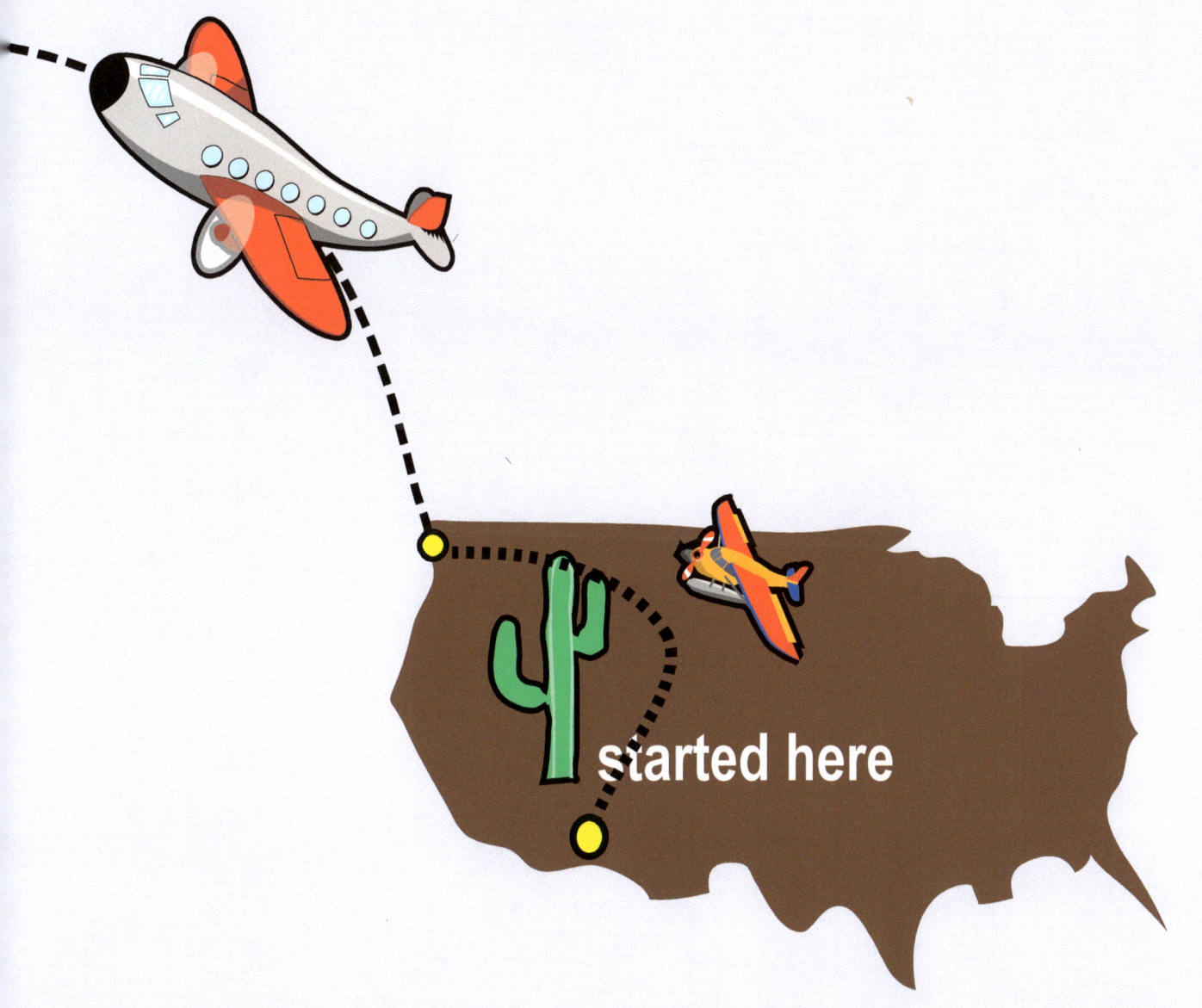

The place where I was born was wonderful. My brothers, my sister and I would play together all day long. We took lots of naps and especially liked to **SNUGGLE,** with our mom.

ONE DAY, a person came and started playing with my brothers and my sister and me. Suddenly, they picked up my brother and looked at him closely.

The person took my **BROTHER** with them, and he was gone. It happened to my sister next. Then my other brother was taken.

Finally, everyone was gone, and it was just me and mom. She didn't seem to mind. It was nice to nap and snuggle with my mom, but playtime was very **LONELY**.

One day a **PERSON** woke me from a warm, cozy nap. Confused, I looked around and learned that this person was Sharon, and she was trying to pick me up.

I got scared that I would be separated from my **MOM** like my brothers and my sister were. There was no place to run or hide. My mom watched me carefully. I noticed a warm, knowing smile on her face.

Sharon reached down and scooped me up. I braced for the **WORST,** but she held me gently in her arms. It was almost like snuggling with my mom.

SHARON came back, picked me up and started taking me away. This did not feel good. We got into a car and started driving. Where were we going?

Why wasn't my **MOM** coming with us? I was getting nervous. Sharon began talking to me and petting me, and I started to calm down.

As I looked out of the **WINDOW,** I had never seen so many new things before. Great smells, cool breezes, lots of activity, and things to explore.

This ride was kind of cool and not that scary after all…in fact this ride was **FUN.** I was starting to like this new adventure. It was very exciting.

Sharon took me to a woman who looked into my **NOSE, EARS,** and **MOUTH.** Then she poked me with something sharp. That hurt, but she gave me some yummy treats that made me forget all about the sharp poke.

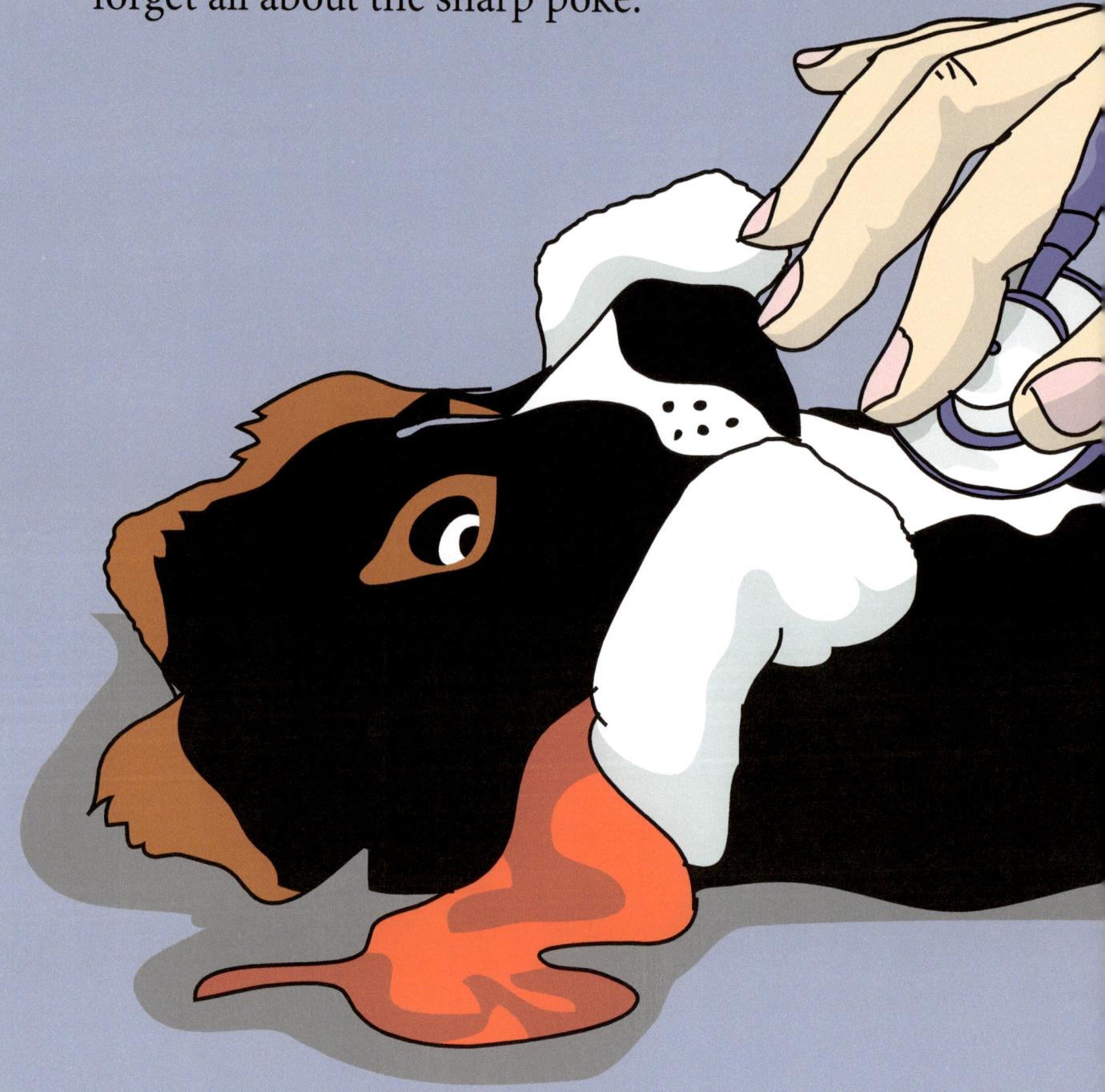

Next, Sharon took me to her home. It was filled with all kinds of new smells, sights, sounds, and room to **PLAY**.

During the night I began thinking of mom in those **QUIET** moments before sleep takes over. Life was getting to be less scary and more fun.

The next morning, Sharon put me into my dog carrier and we went to a **NOISY** place where many people were busy doing all sorts of things—none that looked like puppy play.

The next thing I knew, Sharon was gone, and I was alone. As I watched all of the activity, every once in awhile a person would stop, look in on me and say, "Ooh, what a CUTE puppy!"

Then I was placed onto a small airplane. I settled into a seat before buckling-up. It seemed like a perfect time to curl up and take a **NAP.**

Suddenly, there were loud **NOISES!** I felt my stomach rise, and my ears filled with pressure. What was going on?

I opened my eyes and could see that we were going up into the clouds. I was **FLYING** in an airplane!

A while later the airplane landed with a hard **THUD.** Then a man grabbed me and my carrier and took me to another building, then he set me on some kind of belt. The belt began to move.

I looked around and saw a mass of belts moving in different directions. Each belt held lots of different sized and **SHAPED** boxes.

The belt took me right into a big, **DARK** hole in the side of a big airplane. When the belt stopped and my eyes adjusted to the dark, I noticed that this time there were no seats with people in them.

I felt **ALONE** and frightened. I decided a nap would make me feel much better.

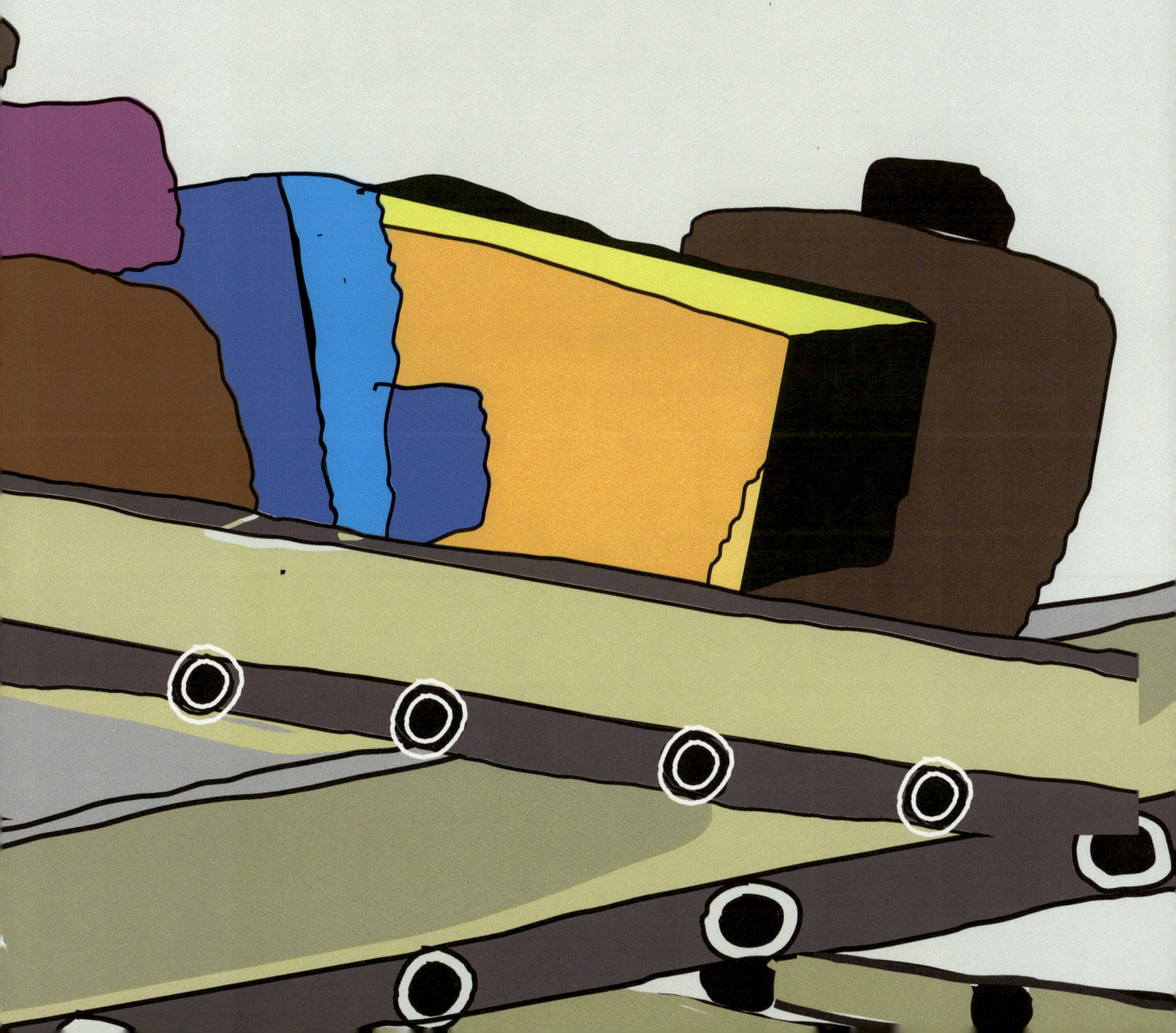

I woke up to the hum of the airplane and a loud hissing noise. I looked around and noticed another carrier like mine next to me on the airplane. I could not believe what I saw—an awful, dreaded **CAT!** The cat's yellow eyes narrowed, and she was yowling and hissing at me.

I barked at her to stop, and I wanted to chase her away, but at first I could not get the carrier door open. She seemed very mean, but then I noticed something.....she looked frightened. I realized that this cat must be **SCARED** and confused, too.

This made me feel a little better, but then the door shut with a **BANG,** and it got very dark. I pressed my body hard against the carrier, trying to get closer to the cat.

She calmed down and huddled **CLOSER** to me, too. I decided that it was better to have a cat for company than to be scared all by myself.

This had been an exciting day with all sorts of new experiences. Now, my eyes felt heavy, and I drifted off into a deep **SLEEP.**

When I **WOKE-UP,** my ears were popping again, and I felt my stomach take a dip. What was happening now?

But in this **DARK,** cold place, all I wanted to do was go back to the safety of my dreams and sleep. I curled up with my blanket, used my fluffy tail for a pillow and tried to fall back asleep.

Before I could drift off to dreamland, the plane jerked and came to a complete **STOP**. What ....next? Suddenly, the door opened, and the sunlight was so bright it hurt my eyes at first.

A man grabbed my carrier and set it **GENTLY** on a conveyor belt. He put the cat right behind me, and we rode together toward a big building.

Dave's daughter, **JENNIFER,** was excited all day about getting a new dog. "It was one of those days," she said, "when time seemed to stand still." Jennifer knew that after school she would be going to the airport to meet her family's newest member.

The school day finally..... ended, and it was time to go pick up the puppy. Dave met Jennifer at school, and she **JUMPED** into the truck. Then they drove the short distance to the airlines' freight pick-up area.

When they arrived, I saw Jennifer run into the building, right up to me on the counter and look right at me. She said, "That is the cutest **PUPPY** I have ever seen!" The people working at the airport were petting and talking to me.

Jennifer looked up in wonder at Dave with her big, **BLUE** eyes and asked, "Can I pick him up?" "You sure can! He is all ours," Dave replied.

I was so **HAPPY** that I could not stop wagging my tail. I knew that this was going to be my new family.

"What should we name him?" Jennifer asked. Mmm...Dave thought for a minute and said, "I think we should name him **COSMOS**. He is a Cowboy Dog and sure did come a long way to be part of our family."

So, that is the story of how I became **COSMOS**, the **COWBOY DOG**, and came to live with a family in Alaska. I have to go now, but next time I will tell you about snow, moose encounters, dog sleds, and all kinds of adventures I have had since moving to the Last Frontier.

Welcome, **COSMOS**, to our home in Alaska on the Last Frontier.

COSMOS'S RULES

LEASH: Rope that attaches to my collar, enabling me to lead Dave wherever I want to go.

DOG BED: Any soft, clean surface, such as the bed in the guest room or the couch in the living room.

DROOL: Liquid which, when combined with my sad eyes, forces Dave to give me his food. Done properly, I must sit as close as I can to Dave and get the drool on him.

SNIFF: Social custom used to greet other dogs, similar to the human exchange of business cards and shaking hands.

GARBAGE CAN: Container put out to test my ingenuity. I must stand on my hind legs and try to push the lid off with my nose. If I do it right, I'm rewarded with all kinds of goodies like butter wrappers to shred, beef bones to consume, and moldy crusts of bread, m......mmm.

CHILDREN: Short people of a great petting height. Standing close to them assures some good petting. When running, they are fun to chase. If they fall down, they are comfortable to sit on.

MORE OF COSMOS'S RULES

DEAFNESS: A condition which affects me when Dave wants me in, and I want to stay out. Symptoms include staring blankly at Dave, running in the opposite direction, and then sitting or lying down.

WASTEBASKET: A cool dog toy filled with paper, envelopes, and old candy wrappers. It is important to evenly distribute its contents throughout the house before Dave comes home.

BATH: When I find something especially good to roll in, Dave gets jealous and uses this degrading form of torture to get even but, I get back by standing next to Dave or the furniture and shake.

LOVE: A feeling of intense affection, given freely and without restriction. The best way of showing my love is to wag my tail and smile. This is also a great way to get love in return.

EPILOGUE

March 9, 2000, Cosmos (Coz) arrived in Anchorage Alaska to become our family's pet. Cosmos loves living on the **"LAST FRONTIER"** in Alaska.

Coz has had some terrific adventures: learning how to walk on ice, play in the snow, herd **MOOSE,** skijor, and even join an Iditarod sled dog mushing team.

His home has a large fenced yard, to keep the moose out and Cosmos in, and it is a great place to play. Part of our family is a Blue Merle Sheltie named **NOVA**, who was born in Alaska and is Coz's best friend, and side-kick.

Cosmos and Nova spend their days roaming their yard and napping, often curled up together in the **SUN.** During the snowy winter they like to spend time playing in the snow.

Cosmos at Sharon's

Cosmos in Alaska

Cosmos at 6 Months

Cosmos Meets Nova

Cosmos & Nova Play

Cosmos in Costume

Cosmos

Cosmos at 10 Years

THE REAL COSMOS WHO LIVES IN ALASKA

www.ingramcontent.com/pod-product-compliance
Lightning Source LLC
Chambersburg PA
CBHW041534040426

42446CB00002B/88